THE DREAM CATCHER

BY JANE A

ILLUSTRATED BY ANTH

FULL FLIGHT

Titles in Full Flight 6

Badger Publishing Limited
15 Wedgwood Gate, Pin Green Industrial Estate,
Stevenage, Hertfordshire SG1 4SU
Telephone: 01438 356907. Fax: 01438 747015.
www.badger-publishing.co.uk
enquiries@badger-publishing.co.uk

The Dream Catcher ISBN 978-1-84691-665-6

Text © Jane A.C. West 2009
Complete work © Badger Publishing Limited 2009

Series Editor: Jonny Zucker
Publisher: David Jamieson.
Editor: Danny Pearson
Design: Fi Grant
Cover illustration: Anthony Williams

THE DREAM CATCHER

CONTENTS

Badger Publishing

CHAPTER 1
BAD DREAMS

It was dark. The room had no windows.
Anoki could not breath.

He tried to bang on the door,
but he couldn't move.

He tried to shout for help,
but he couldn't speak.

"Aaaaaaaaagh!"

Anoki woke up suddenly.

In the early morning light, his fear
faded away.

"Not again," he said to himself.
"I've had that nightmare three times."

Each nightmare had been the same:
the dark room, not being able to move,
not being able to speak.

Anoki stared at the dream catcher.

It hung in his window, moving gently
in the breeze.

"Dad should ask for his money back,"
said Anoki.

"That dream catcher doesn't work!"

The dream catcher was round and made of wood. It was covered in threads, a bit like a spider's web. Feathers hung under it.

Anoki's Dad had brought it back from America for him.

"It was made by a real American Indian," said his Dad.

"It's called a dream catcher. It catches bad dreams in the web. Good dreams slide down the feathers and into you while you're asleep."

"Sounds cool!" said Anoki.

"It's just a story," said his Dad,
"it doesn't really work."

"Dad was right about that," said Anoki.

Anoki went down to breakfast.
His Dad was reading the paper.

"The price of heating has gone up again," said his Dad.

Anoki grunted.

"And they haven't found that missing
man yet - the rich millionaire,"
said his Dad.

"Is there any good news in that paper?"
said Anoki.

CHAPTER 2
THE FACE IN THE MIRROR

It was dark. The room had no windows.
Anoki could not breath.

He tried to bang on the door,
but he couldn't move.

He tried to shout for help,
but he couldn't speak.

The door opened. Light flooded in.
A voice spoke.

"Tell me what I want to know and I'll
let you go."

Anoki shook his head.

"Tell me what I want to know or else..."

A knife touched Anoki's face.

The blade was cold on his skin.

He saw his scared face in the mirror - but it wasn't his face. It was a man's face.

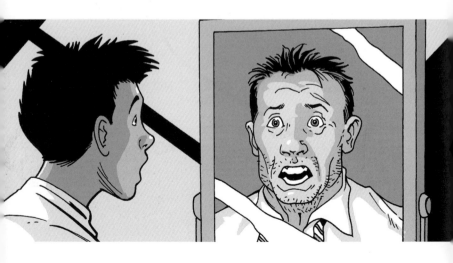

Anoki woke up. His heart pounding. Anoki knew the face in his dream: it had been on TV and in the papers.

It was the face of the missing millionaire.

Anoki scowled at the dream catcher. "You are giving me nightmares," he said.

He tore down the dream catcher and threw it in a drawer.

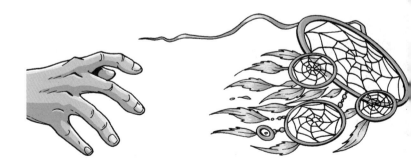

CHAPTER 3
REAL DREAMS

It was dark. The room had no windows.
Anoki could not breath.

He tried to bang on the door,
but he couldn't move.

He tried to shout for help,
but he couldn't speak.

The door opened. Light flooded in.
A voice spoke.

"Tell me where the diamonds are."

Anoki shook his head.

"Tell me what I want to know or else…"

Anoki woke up. His heart was racing.

Anoki turned to look at his window. The dream catcher was moving gently in the breeze.

"But I put you in the drawer!" he said.

"You look tired," said Anoki's Dad at breakfast. "Didn't you sleep well?"

Anoki shook his head.

"I keep having nightmares about that kidnapped millionaire. Someone with a knife keeps asking him about diamonds."

Anoki's Dad stared at him.

"How did you know he'd been kidnapped," said Anoki's dad.
"And how did you know it was to do with diamonds?

"The police only told the newspapers this morning."

"You won't believe me," said Anoki.

"Try me," said his Dad.

Anoki took a deep breath.
"I've been having these nightmares,"
he said.

"I dream that I'm locked in a room.
I can't move and I can't speak.
When I look in a mirror, it's not my
face - it's the face of that missing
millionaire.

The person with a knife keeps saying,
'Tell me where the diamonds are... or
else'.

Then I wake up."

Anoki paused.

"Dad, I think it's to do with that
dream catcher.

It's like… it's like the
dream catcher is sending this man's
dreams to me - except they're not
dreams, they're nightmares - and
they're real."

"That's impossible," said Anoki's Dad.

"I know, Dad," said Anoki.
"But that's what's happening."

CHAPTER 4
NOTHING BUT THE TRUTH

The sign outside said 'Police'.

"Are you ready?" said Anoki's Dad.

Anoki nodded. He didn't feel ready. He felt stupid. The police would never believe him.

"Listen, son," said the policeman. "Lots of kids have dreams about bad things but it's not a police matter."

"He knew about the diamonds before it was in the papers," said Anoki's Dad.

"I don't know how he knew - he just did."

"Sir, wasting police time is a serious matter," said the policeman.

"Wait a minute," said the policewoman. "Can you describe the face you saw in the mirror?"

"He had dark hair, dark eyes and he hadn't shaved for a few days."

The policeman looked cross.

"His photo has been in the paper," he said.

Anoki tried to think.

"He had a small scar above his eyebrow. And he was wearing a gold chain. The chain had something on it... a symbol."

The two police officers looked at each other.

"Can you draw it?"
said the policewoman.

She handed Anoki some paper.
He drew an arrow on it.

"It looked like this," he said.

"How did you know that?" said the policeman.

"We haven't told anyone about that gold chain. That information is top secret."

"I told you," said Anoki.

"I saw it in my dream!"

"Tell me the truth!" shouted the policeman.

"He's told you!" said Anoki's Dad.

"Take it easy," said the policewoman. "He's just a kid."

"My son is not a liar!" said Anoki's Dad.

"Quiet!" shouted the policeman. "Or I will arrest you."

"I know why you're here. You think you can get a reward for helping the police. But you're not fooling me!"

They made Anoki and his Dad answer the same questions over and over again.

In the end they let them go, but Anoki could tell that they didn't believe him.

As they left the police station, Anoki looked over his shoulder.
The angry policeman was watching them. His face was as cold as stone.

CHAPTER 5
FLIGHT OR FIGHT

Anoki was tired. They'd been at the
police station for hours.

He fell asleep in the car.

It was dark. The room had no windows.
Anoki could not breath.

He tried to bang on the door,
but he couldn't move.

He tried to shout for help,
but he couldn't speak.

The door opened. Light flooded in.

"Where are the diamonds?"
said the woman.

Anoki stared past the woman and out
of the window.

He could see the electric sign
'Hartley's'. He knew that sign. It was
oppposite the cinema in town.

Anoki woke up suddenly.

"Dad!" he shouted.

But it was too late. Their car was hit
from behind by a large van.

They skidded across the road and the
car flipped over.

Glass broke and metal screeched.

Anoki was lying upside down.

He could see blood on his Dad's face.

"Dad!" he cried. "Dad!"

Anoki was pulled from the car.
A torch was shining in his face.

"Tell me where the diamonds are,"
said the voice, "or I'll kill your Dad."

Anoki stared into the face of the
policewoman.
Her mouth was twisted in anger,
and she held a gun.

CHAPTER 6
FIGHTING BACK

"Tell me what you know, or I'll kill your Dad," she snarled.

Anoki's mouth was dry.

"Police! Drop your weapon!" shouted a voice in the darkness.
"We've got you surrounded!"

The woman grabbed Anoki.
"Let me go or I'll kill the kid," she shouted.

"You're not going anywhere. Let the kid go. Now!"

Anoki knew what to do.

He bit the woman's hand hard.

She screamed and dropped her gun.

The policeman walked towards them.

"Well done, son," he said smiling.

"You were very brave. I'm sorry I gave you a hard time in the police station, but we've suspected PWC Mason for a long time. We followed her when she left the police station."

He put handcuffs on the woman.

"Tell us where the millionaire is," he said.

"Never!" she said.

Anoki took a deep breath.
"I know where he is," he said.

CHAPTER 7
BLUE ICE

The missing millionaire was found just where Anoki had dreamed he would be.

"How did you know where I was?" he said.

"I dreamt about you," said Anoki.

"I guess you know where I hid the diamonds, too," said the man, smiling.

"I didn't dream that bit," said Anoki. "That would have been a good dream. I only had bad dreams."

The man looked at Anoki.

"Yes. They were very bad dreams. But because of them, you saved my life. Thank you."

Anoki smiled. "I didn't dream about diamonds but I did dream about your gold chain," he said.

The man gave him a strange look. "Do you know what this arrow on my chain means?" the man said.

Anoki shook his head.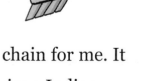

"My wife bought this chain for me. It was made by an American Indian. The arrow is a sign of protection."

Anoki stared.

"I think it protected me," said the man, "with your help."

Anoki nodded slowly. It was hard to believe.

"Now," said the man. "Would you like to see what £1 million of diamonds looks like?"

He unwrapped a small bag made of black velvet.

The diamonds glittered like blue ice.